Statues Of New York City

Jack Byard

CONTENTS

ACKNOWLEDGEMENTS

Many thanks to my family, my wife Elaine, my daughters Ruth and Karen and my granddaughter Rebecca for their constant help and support.

Many thanks also to the Library of Congress, the Smithsonian Institute, the New York Public Library and the Garment District Alliance for all their help in my research.

Special thanks must go to Brecht Bug, my eyes on the ground in New York City, without whose help and expert knowledge this book would not have been feasible.

PHOTOGRAPH CREDITS

(3) Kevin Hackert, (23) Zack Lee (24) Jag 9889.
All other images Brecht Bug via Flickr.

107TH INFANTRY MEMORIAL

Description:

Height of figures 9'11" (2.5lm) overall height 17°6" (5.34m) length 32 8" (9.96m) depth 10 (3.05m).

This heroic bronze group depicts seven World War I soldiers in battle. The soldiers are poised on a North Jay granite platform, the architects Rogers & Háneman and the sculptor Karl Morningstar Illava who drew on his personal experiences as serving sergeant with the107 th, the soldiers hands are models of his own. This was a regiment of the New York Army National Guard and was in action until 1993.

The Doughboys are set for action, ready to advance from the woodland surrounding Central Park. Doughboys, the nickname of the infantry in World War I were often teenagers, its origins are unclear.

In World War II the Doughboys became the G.Is The lead infantryman of the group was said to have been based on boxing hero Genc Tunney, bt was denied by the officers as the figures were typical of the soldiers in the field of battle.

The monument was dedicatéd on September 29th 1927, a date chosen to commemorate the 9th anniversary of the Battle of St. Quentin Canal when the regiment attacked the Hindenburg Line.

The sons of two fallen soldiers Captain Clinton E. Fisk and Captain Fancher Nicoll unveiled the monument.

SEVENTH REGIMENT NEW YORK
ONE HUNDRED AND SEVENTH INFANTRY

ALEXANDER HAMILTON

Description:

Height 155" (4.70m) on an integral plinth on a pedestal 7'10" (2.40m) square.

The Westerly granite statue can be seen on East Drive opposite 83rd Street dressed in the basic clothing of Colonial times. The sculptor was Carl H Corads, he used a bust of Hamilton sculpted by Giuseppe Ceracchi as a model for the head.

The statue was presented to the city by his son, John C. Hamilton in 1880, Hamilton was born in the West Indies on the island of Nevis into not the wealthiest families and in 1772, as an ophan, arrived in the US in his mid-teens.

He was educated at King's College, now Columbia University, and whilst still a teenager he volunteered to serve in the Revolutionary Wars witha New York Artillery Company, he rose to the rank of captain, And later as a Lieutenant Colonel was aide-de-camp and secretary to General George Washington, in 1780 he married Elizabeth Schuyler a member ofa prominent New York Family. Hamilton was the first U.S, Secretary of Treasury. His face appears on the S10 bill the only man, apart from Benjamin Franklin, to appear on a US bill, who was not a president.

For 30 years he was a resident of New York, on his retirement, he built a house, the only home he ever owned, in what is now known as Hamilton Heights, moderm-day Harlem. I must not forget the hit Broadway musical, Hamilton

ATLAS

Description:

Atlas figure height 15ft (4.6m). Statue plus plinth 45ft (14m). Weight approximately 7 tons (6400 kg).

The bronze muscular statue of Atlas can be found across 5th Avenue from St. Patrick's Cathedral balanced on a powerful left leg the right leg is locked in place on the rear edge of the plinth to prevent his knees buckling whilst keeping the heavens aloft, this was his punishment for leading the Titans into battle against the gods for control of the heavens.

The magnificent statue was designed by sculptor Lee Lawrie in collaboration with architectural modeller and sculptor Rene Paul Chambellan, it is the largest sculpture within the 22 acre Rockefeller Centre and was unveiled in 1937.

It is said that on the unveiling there were strong protests from the Italian community of New York, their grievance was that the statue bore a remarkable resemblance to the fascist ruler of Italy, Benito Mussolini. The statue has appeared in the television series 30 Rock.

BAILEY FOUNTAIN

Description:

Height 25" (7.62 m) with basin diameter 120 (37 m)

Created in 1932 this bronze Art Deco design of the Bailey fountain consists of six monumental figures beginning with the top two, a man representing wisdom with his left hand on the tiller steering the ship of life and a woman representing felicity with her right hand holdinga cornucopia. Below them are two other statues, one a chubby standing child helping to shoulder that cornucopia while the second is a laughing mythological figure called neteus who is the eldest son of Pontus the Sea and Gaia the earth.

To the sides of the fountain are the two remaining aqustic merimen figures with upper torsos emerging from the water, their heads back blowing conch shells as their fish tails twist in the background. This fountain is located in the true centre of grand amy plaza and was sculpted by eugene savsge from the design of architects Edgerton Swarthout and H. Crig severance and was narmed for the Brooklyn philanthropist Frank Bailey and his wife Mary Louise.

This is the fourth fountain to be located in grand amy plaza the first was called the fountain of the golden spray in 1867 and consisted of a single jet of water shooting skyward.

The second was called the dome fountain in 1873 and conssted of a two tier double dormne structure of cast iron with 24 coloured glass windows designed by architect Calvernt Vaux the third was called the electric fountain in 1897 and worked in a similar manner as the dancing waters AKA the Bellagio Casino Fountain" in current day Las Vegas, Nevada.

In 1915 this third fountain's underground working were demolished to make way for construction of the New York city subway's IRT Eastern Parkway Line train numbers 2,3,4 and 5.

BALTO

Description:

Nose to tail 4' 6" (1.40m) Height 2' 6" (0.79m)

The bronze statue of Balto the Siberian Husky was sculpted by Frederick George Richard Roth and can be found standing on a natural boulder of Manhattan Schist near East Drive at 67th Street.It was cast and dedicated in 1925, and Balto himself was present.

The back and ears of Balto are well burnished, for almost 100 years young children and very mature children have sat on his back stroking his ears possibly hoping to feel the strength and courage of this amazing dog. In 1925 Nome a city in Alaska suffered an outbreak of Diptheria, a disease I know too well. The city had a population of 1,429 and only sufficient antitoxin serum for 300.

The city was icebound with no access by road rail or air, 20 teams of dog sledges were bought in, and one team of dogs was led by Balto. The teams were facing blizzards and temperatures of -23F (-31c).

Balto's team and the other teams had a 25 mile journey. The musher was unable to see for a major part of the journey because of the blizzard and it was left to Balto to navigate to Nome. The serum arrived safely, it was defrosted. The epidemic was over. Only five people died. Many mushers and dogs were decorated for gallantry. Balto is the face, representing more than 100 dogs that took place in the heroic medicine delivery. Balto crossed the Rainbow Bridge in 1933, aged 14 years.

BETHESDA FOUNTAIN- ANGEL OF THE WATERS

Description:

The Angel height 8' Height including plinth 26' (7.92m). Diameter 96'(29.26m).

The bronze statue is to celebrate the opening of the Croton Aqueduct in 1842 bringing fresh clean water to New York City and is based on the story of the blessing of the waters in Saint John's Gospel.

Manhattan was surrounded by brackish rivers, creating many health problems. The bronze angel was designed by Emma Stebbins, the first woman in New York City to receive a major commission. The statue base was designed by architect Calvert Vaux with further detail by English born architect Jacob Wrey Mould. The Angel of the Waters can be seen touching down with the delicacy of a ballet dancer and in her hand the symbol of purity, a lily.

The four cherubs represent peace, purity, health and temperance. The fountain is fed by freshwater from the Croton Aqueduct. The large pool is constructed of polished Westerly Granite and the smaller upper pool is made of BlueStone.

CHESTER A. ARTHUR

Description:

Satue Height 9' 2" (2.79m) and Pedestal 9' (2.74m) square.

The bronze statue of the 2l st United States President Chester Alan Arhur was created by sculptor George Edwin Bissell in 1898 and stands looking South on the East side of Madison Square Park near 26th Street and Madison Avenue. Arthur was born in Fairfield, Vermont grejv up in upstate New York and practiced law in New York City.

He served as quartermaster general of the New York Militia during the American Civil War. Following the war, hedevoted more time to New York Republican politics and quickly rose in Senator Roscoe Conkling's political organization. President Ulysses S. Grant appointed him to the post of Collector of the Port of New York in 1871 and he was an important supporter of Conkling and the Stalwart faction of the Republican Party.

In 1878, President Rutherford B. Hayes fired Arthur as part of a plan to reform the federal patronage system in New York. Garfield won the Republican nomination for president in 1880, and Arthur was nominated for vice president to balance the ticket as an Eastern Stalwart.

Four months into his term, Garfield was shot by an assassin, he died 1l weeks later, and Arthur assumed the Presidency Arhur's monument was unveiled on June 13th 1899 and not long after the unveiling, vandals climbed the statue and removed the bronze eyeglasses from the right hand of the President.

George E. Bissell recast the spectacles and these, too, were promptly stolen. A third pair of rims were then modelled and cast in bronze, and these were placed securely in the right hand, and stolen again in 1912, making the hand an enigma as to its pose.

CHRISTOPHER COLUMBUS

Description:

The overall monument is 76'(32.1m). The Columbus statue is 13' (3.9m). Made from Carrara marble it stands on top of a 35' (10.6m) granite column which rests on a 26' (6.9m) pedestal with an angel gazing at a world globe on the Southside and a bronze bird of prey on the Northside. Below both are additional bronze relief sculptural scenes reenacting Columbus' first standing on the shores of the Americas.

The statue, sculpted by Gaetano Russo, can be seen at the centre of Columbus Circle Manhattan. It was erected in 1892 to commemorate the 400th anniversary of Columbus landing in America.

The money raised to build this magnificent monument was contributed by Italian businesses throughout the U.S. led by Carlo Barsotti and the II Progresso Italian American newspaper of New York. Bronze decorations representing the Columbus ships Nina, Pinta, Santa Maria are attached to the sides of the main column and were cast in Rome at the Nelli Foundry.

During the 1920s construction of the Eighth Avenue subway, the Columbus statue was moved 2" (5cm) North and developed a list of 1.5" (3.8cm). Restoration and cleaning of the monument occurred in 1934 and again in 1992.

CIVIC VIRTUE

Description:

17 (5.3m)

This marble work of art is now possibly in its final resting place, the Green-Wood cemetery. It has, from its first day, been a statuc of controversy. The fountain was commissioned by Mayor George B. McClellan in 1909.

It was funded by a bequest by Angelina Crane a New York socialite. Civic Virtue was created by sculptor Frederick William Mc Monnies and architect Thomas Hastings, carved by the Piccirilli brothers and unveiled in 1922.

The well-muscled male nude stands on a square pedestal with dolphin heads spewing water into the pool. Civic Virtue has a sword resting on his shoulder above two prone females In 1920 women had been given the right to vote and the statuctyas seen as misogynistic. Fiorello H. La Guardia was mayor from 1924-1934 who nicknamed the sculpture 'Fat Boy' and disliked seeing the naked buttocks every day from his office, Mayor La Guardia gave it to Queens in 1941 when they built the new City Hall.

It was a focal point for several feminist demonstrations and it fell into disrepair and was moved, without the pedestal and base, to the cemetery and restored.

Let us for a moment look at the quality of the carving, imagine the pen in your hand is a chisel and imagine how long it would take you to create this work of art.

DOUBLE CHECK

Description:

Lifesize, weight ?

Who can ever forget 9/11

Mountains of grey ash covered the ruins of Liberty Park, as the grey ash and debris settled groups of emergency responders looked across the field of debris and spotted a dazed, grey dust-covered survivor. As they worked their way towards the figure they realised it was a statue.

In 1982 the sculptor, Michael Seward Johnson II created the bronze Double Check statue. It was on loan to Merrill Lynch who displayed it in Liberty Plaza Park in the Financial District. A businessman checking the contents of his briefcase before going to a meeting. The recovered businessman had been knocked from his base, he was a little knocked about and scratched but he went straight to the hearts of the New Yorkers.

The Double Check was now a memorial to the 3000 who lost their lives whilst just earning a living, to take care of their families. He now sits on a marble bench in Liberty Plaza Park facing the site of the towers. He was cleaned and refurbished by the sculptor, the scratches, bumps and bruises were left as a reminder.

DRUMMER BOY

Description:

Height overall 10' (32.80m), the Drummer Boy 6' 4" (1.93m)

The statue and plinth are made entirely of white zinc statue of Clarence D, MacKenzie created in 1878, a drummer boy of the Thirteenth Regiment, New York State Militia.

Most of the metal monuments in Green-Wood cemetery were produced by The Monumental Bronze Company of Bridgeport, Connecticut, He was the first resident of Brooklyn to die in the Civil War. His memorial can be found in the section donated by the Green-Wood Cemetery, along Linden Avenue, for Civil War soldiers and veterans.

The Drummer Boy has recently been restored by the cemetery for $15000. Clarence was stationed in Annapolis Maryland and had finished his daily duties, he was asleep in his tent, there was practice rifle fire in the distance. One round of misaimed fire tore into his tent, Clarence was killed.

He was 12 years old. A message to his mother shortly before he died, *"Dear mother, do not cry for me, for I am well off, and I hope to return to you in three months or sooner. Your Clarry"*. Clarence MacKenzie's funeral was held on July 14th 1861 with 3,000 mourners in attendance.

DRUMMER BOY

ELEANOR ROOSEVELT

Description:

Height 8' (2.44m)

This bronze and Belfast black granite statue of a memorable lady, the 32nd First Lady of the US, 1946-1952, a diplomat an activist and a humanitarian can be found on 72nd Street and Riverside Drive. It is believed to be the only monument to an American Presidents wife.

The memorial was designed by Bruce Kelly and David Varnell, and Penelope Jencks sculpted the monument and Michael Middleton Dwyer created the boulder and footstone. It is surrounded by a granite block pavement.

The appearance is pensive and neither young nor old. Eleanor Roosevelt is 'surrounded' by three oak trees giving the impression she is resting and contemplating in a woodland area. The placing of the memorial was a major part of the project.

Born in New York and educated in England. After helping in her husband's successful Presidential campaign she fully embraced the role of First Lady.

Eleanor Roosevelt championed and supported various schemes to alleviate unemployment and poverty and fight the cause of racial equality. Later with the United Nations, she led the body that drafted the Universal Declaration of Human Rights and was involved with the American Red Cross and the Womens Trade Union. "Her Glow has warmed the world" Adlai E. Stevenson.

FATHER DUFFY

Description:

Statue height 7' 6" pedestal 4' 10" square and 10' high.

The bronze figure of Father Duffy, was designed by the New York sculptor Charles Keck, and rests against a Celtic cross and plinth made of Archean green granite in Times Square. Francis P. Duffy was born in Ontario Canada in 1871 and ordained in 1896 moving to New York in1898 and for a while taught at the College of St Joseph's Seminary training priests for the Arch Diocese of New York. Lieutenant Francis P. Duffy's military career began in 1898 as a chaplain in the Spanish American Civil War.

In World War 1 he was with the 165th US Infantry, the Old 69th New York. He was never far from the centre of the action in the fields and trenches and accompanied the stretcher-bearers rescuing and comforting the wounded and the dying and he buried the dead. His actions and bravery were recognised, he was awarded the Distinguished Service Cross, Distinguished Service Medal, Conspicuous Service Cross, (New York State), The Legion d'Honneur, and the Croix de Guerre.

He was the United States army's most decorated cleric. After WWI he became the pastor of Holy Cross Church at 237 W. 42nd Street ministering to actors, producers and longshoremen.

PLAY
NPR
FATHER DUFFY

FIORELLO LA GUARDIA

Description:

Statue 6'4" (1.93m)   Pedestal Height 3'2" (0.96m) width 3'4" (1.02m)

This bronze statue created by the architect Ruth Shapiro and sculptor Neil Estem is bursting with life. Fiorello, nicknamed "Little Flower" the translation of Fiorello, standing on a granite plinth holding forth.

Born in 1882 in Greenwich Village the son of a United States Army bandleader. Fiorello was admitted to the bar in 1910 after gaining a law degree at New York University.   In 1916 he became the first United States Italian-American Congressman where for 16years he held many posts.

He was elected the Lord Mayor serving from 1933-1945, taking over from Mayor James J. Walker who was forced from office following many scandals. Mayor La Guardia was elected on a Fusion ticket, an arrangement where two or more political parties on a ballot list the same candidate. He created a quality transport service, parks, bridges and airports and cracked down on illegal gambling. During his third term, 1942-1945 Grace Mansion became the official residence of the New York Mayor.

In the 1990s friends of La Guardia Place raised funds and commissioned a statue, several artists submitted designs and the commission was given to Neil Estem. The statue was dedicated in 1994.

FIORELLO H. LAGUARDIA
MAYOR OF NEW YORK CITY
1934 — 1945

GARMENT WORKER

Description:

Height 8' (2.44m) base: Black marble 4'x4'x1' (129.90 x 30.50 cm square).

The bronze statue, of a Jewish immigrant worker in his work clothes and yarmulke, bent over a Singer sewing machine, his feet on the treadle concentrating on `every stitch. This true representation is in the likeness of the sculptor, Judith Weller, whose father was in the garment industry. J

udith Weller was born in Israel and first came to the USA in 1957 as an exchange student, three years later she submitted a 24" high sculpture, to the National Sculpture Society of a garment worker at his work, the worker was a mirror image of her father, it was created to commemorate the Jewish garment workers.

The sculpture was admired by a member of the Ladies Garment Workers Union and, working with Judith Weller sponsored the 8-foot statue on a black marble base we admire today in the garment district.

The $35,000 cost was sponsored by forty-three unions, garment manufacturers and many well-known designers and banks. This evocative figure creates many different feelings. It may be seen at 555 7th Avenue.

GREGORYS
COFFEE

GENERAL PHILIP HENRY SHERIDAN

Description:

Height 12' 4" (3.76m) square 3' 10" (1.17m).

The Bronze statue of General Philip Sheridan, a distinguished Civil War Commander, standing on a Conway green granite plinth. The General was only small 5'5" (1.65m) but he was a giant of a man and commander.

The figure was sculpted by Joseph P. Pollia, it was cast and dedicated in 1936. The money was raised through a public subscription. The General can be found watching over Christopher Park, Grove and West 4th Streets. Philip Henry Sheridan was born in Albany in 1831, the third of six children of an Irish immigrant family. He worked in a general dry goods store as a clerk and bookkeeper. He obtained an appointment to the United States Military Academy at West Point from a store customer in 1848.

Five years later, after a bumpy journey, he was created a brevet, a name given because there were insufficient regular army officers, 2nd Lieutenant in the 1st infantry. In 1861 he was promoted to captain and made Chief Quartermaster and Commissary of the army S.W. Missouri. Life was not easy.

In 1862 he was promoted to Colonel of the 2nd Michigan Cavalry. On June 1st 1888 he was promoted to General and died two months later.

GENERAL PHILIP HENRY
SHERIDAN

GENERAL SHERMAN

Description:

The statue height 17' 6" (5.33m) and stands atop a granite 25' 4" (7.72 m) high granite pedestal. The distance from the front step to the rear step is 59' 8" (18.19m).

You are in the Grand Army Plaza on 59th Street and 5th Avenue opposite the Plaza Hotel gazing at the glittering statue of General Sherman which is covered with 23.75k of pure gold leaf. General William Tecumseh Sherman the American Civil War general, was born in Ohio in 1820 and died in New York in 1891.

General Sherman had many friends in the City's Chamber of Commerce and after his death in 1891 it was agreed that the finance would be raised to create the monument. The sculptor Augustus Saint Gaudens was commissioned to create the monument showing the Generals horse, Ontario, being led by the goddess of victory, Nike.

The model for the goddess was Harriet Eugenia Anderson a friend and companion of Augustus Saint Gaudens. The sculptor became seriously ill during this period and as a result, the commission took 10 years to complete and was dedicated in 1903. The beautiful and robust pedestal on which General Sherman rests was designed by the architect Charles McKim and is made of pink granite.

The monument is located in Sherman Plaza, which is at the intersection of 15th Street NW, Pennsylvania Avenue NW, and Treasury Place NW. The equestrian statue of General Sherman is 17 feet 6 inches (5.33 m) tall, and stands atop a granite pedestal 25 feet 4 inches (7.72 m) high.

GEORGE M. COHAN

Description:

Statue height 8' 7" (2.61m) and pedestal height 6' 11" (2.11m) standing in a square basin of flowers and shrubs

The George M. Cohan bronze figure was created by Sculptor Georg John Lober and dedicated in 1959 in Duffy Square near the intersection of Broadway and 7th Avenue, the centre of Times Square. Cohan was born in Providence, Rhode Island in 1878 into a stage family appearing in both vaudeville and the "legitimate theatre". The Cohan family musical comedy act was known as "The Four Cohans".

Beginning with Little Johnny Jones in 1904, he wrote, composed, produced, and appeared in more than three dozen Broadway musicals. Cohan wrote more than 50 shows and published more than 300 songs becoming one of the leading Tin Pan Alley songwriters, including the standards "Forty-Five Minutes from Broadway", "The Yankee Doodle Boy" and "Give My Regards to Broadway". Cohan was called "the greatest single figure the American theatre ever produced – as a player, playwright, actor, composer and producer".

In 1940, President Franklin Delano Roosevelt presented him with the Congressional Gold Medal for his contributions to World War I morale, in particular with the songs "You're a Grand Old Flag" and "Over There".

GEORGE
• M •
COHAN
1878–1942
Give my Regards to Broadway
tkts

GIANT NEEDLE THREADING A BUTTON

Description:

Needle Length 31' (9.45m) Needle Eye Opening 2' (0.61m) Button Diameter 14' (4.27m)

Created in 1996 by the custom metal works firm of Treitel-Gratz Co, the giant needle and button's fabrication was overseen by Shop Manager Hugh Alexander Cosman (b.1952 - d.2020) and is an excellent example of what is known as Roadside America or Novelty Architecture.

Formerly Architecture due to the now closed and demolished Fashion Centre Information Kiosk no longer at the base of the button and Novelty due to the outsized icons of sewing that represent the Industry of the surrounding neighbourhood known as The Garment District.

The creation of this structure is more akin to signage than an abstract artistic statement. The Needle and Button were inspired by a 16' diameter button sculpture currently located on the campus of The University of Pennsylvania titled "The Split Button" designed by Swedish sculptor Claes Oldenburg. Promotion of the Garment District to tourists and New York natives is the direct reason the Needle and Button were installed at this 7th Avenue and 39th Street corner location.

As mentioned above the removed Information Kiosk no longer exists due to its structural instability. A silver metal tripod representing thread has replaced the kiosk and opened up more pedestrian space for admiring Needle and Button from a new perspective.

WELL

GIUSEPPE GARIBALDI

Description:

Height 20' 8" (6.30m) 10' square (3.05m)

The statue of Giuseppe Garibaldi and the Sword of Italian Unification, was sculpted by Giuseppe Turini and cast in 1888 by the Henry Bonnard Bronze Company. He stands on a square granite pedestal in Washington Square Park in Manhattan.

Garibaldi was a 19th-century Italian patriot. He became a member of the Young Italy Society an Italian nationalist organisation operated by Giuseppe Mazzini. This was the first Republican uprising to create an independent Genoa. It failed and Giuseppe fled to South America where he lived for 12 years fighting against Juan Manuel de Rosas in the Uruguayan Civil War.

He returned to his homeland in 1844 to support Mazzini in the Roman Republic. This was short-lived and he fled to America living on Staten Island with another Italian ex-pat, inventor Antonio Meucci. Garibaldi worked as a candlemaker whilst planning his next military intervention. He almost single-handedly united northern and southern Italy allowing King Victor Emmanuel II of Piedmont to establish the Kingdom of Italy.

The statue was moved in 1970 to allow for work in Washington Square, a glass container was found containing documents about Garibaldi's death and the fund-raising for the statue.

GARIBALDI
1807 — 1882

GIUSEPPE VERDI

Description:

Height 25' 9" (7.85 mm) Diameter 18' (5.5 mm)

The Carrara marble statue of composer Giuseppe Verdi was created by Italian sculptor Pasquale Civiletti in 1906 and is located on West 73rd Street, Broadway and Amsterdam Avenue.

The park area was officially renamed Verdi Square in 1921. The pedestal contains four operatic character figures based on Verdi's works representing Aide, Otello, Leonora of La Forza del Destino and Falstaff. These statues respectively face North, East, South, and West with four large marble lyre stringed instruments placed between them and a time capsule hidden beneath the entire structure.

The Verdi monument was unveiled on October 12th 1906, the 414th anniversary of Columbus's discovery of America. The day began with a march of Italian societies from Washington Square to the site at Broadway and West 73rd Street.

Over 10,000 people attended the unveiling, showing and celebrating the significance of the uniting of the Italian-Americans and their cultural and artistic heritage. The sculptures were unveiled by the grandchild of the president of the Verdi Monument Committee, Carlo Barsotti (1850–1927), pulling the string that released a helium balloon, lifting the monument's red, white and green shroud (the colours of the Italian flag).

A dozen doves concealed in the folds of the shroud were released and flowers cascaded from the veil upon the participants. Decades later the monument suffered from pollution and neglect but in June 1996 a permanent monument maintenance endowment was established by Bertolli USA, Inc.

VERDI

HANS CHRISTIAN ANDERSON

Description:

Height 9'67" (289.56 cm) Width 6' 1" (185.42 cm) Depth 6' 2" (187.96 cm). The bench Height: 3' 1" (99 cm) Width 21' 2" (645.16 cm)   Depth: 17'4" (528.32 cm) Duckling: 1' 10.5" (57.15 cm)

The bronze statue of Hans Christian Andersen 1805-1875, can be found at the edge of the Conservatory Water in Central Park, Anderson is seated on a Stony Creek pink polished granite bench with his top hat beside him.

He is reading his story The Ugly Duckling to a passing duckling. The statue was created by Georg John Lober and cast by the Modern Art Foundry. The statue was funded by the Danish American Women's Association, with help from Danish and American schoolchildren who worked to raise the money to fund the project. It has been a background for many children's reading events.

Since 1957 every Saturday during the summer Children gather around the statue to hear his and other writers' stories. The first story was read by Victor Borge, and many other performers followed in his path. 1973, to the shock and horror of New York, the duckling was stolen. It was recovered and restored.

Children are welcome to climb on the statue to cuddle and touch Hans, the book is highly polished by the number of children who have sat there to have photographs taken by delighted parents

JOHN WATTS

Description:

Height 9' 3" Pedestal 7'

This imposing bewigged bronze judicially robed figure is of John Watts Jr. sculpted by George E. Bissell, erected in 1892. The commission was executed by his grandson General John Watts DePeyster who was concerned his grandfather would be forgotten by the people of Manhattan. John Watts Jr. was the only former British official to hold an American office.

In 1791 he was elected to the New York State Assembly and two years later to the United States Congress. Unfortunately Watts' personal life suffered multiple tragedies with his wife and 10 of his 11 children dying before their time. Watts Jr had a life-long friend in John George Leake, who married Watts's younger sister, Margaret.

When Leake's only son, John George, died at the age of eight in 1793, Leake formulated a plan to carry on his name. He proposed to leave Watts's only surviving son, Robert, his vast fortune. The only caveat being Robert would have to change his surname to Leake. He inheriting his uncle's estate upon Leake's death in 1827.

Ironically, shortly after the will was settled Robert died of congestion of the lungs. Robert left no will and died unmarried so his father Watts Jr become his son's heir. Already wealthy, John Watts Jr had no need for the Leake fortune so he founded the New York Dispensary and the Leake and Watts Orphan House, a charity that still exists as "Leake and Watts Services". His grandsons efforts were thus not in vain for John Watts Jr's statue still remains steadfast in Trinity Church yard.

The sculpture stands as a testament to all public monumental figures that appear to be obscure in the eyes of modern viewers, as if to say "If you don't know who I am, look me up!"

JOHN WATTS

KNEELING FIREMAN

Description:

Height 9' (2.74m), length 12' (3.66m) width 5ft (1.52m) weight 3,000 lb (1360.80 kg).

In October 2000, the Firefighters Association of Missouri had worked hard to design a suitable memorial for the firefighters who had lost their lives on duty.

Through the Matthews International Corporation Bryan Hunt, the sculptor created the bronze Kneeling Fireman and cast it in the companies foundry in Parma, Italy. It was crated up ready for delivery, and arrived at Kennedy Airport, to wait for customs clearance delayed because of the 9/11 attack.

The statue was presented as a gift to all New York residents and was mounted on a granite pedestal, a gift from the Milstein family. The memorial was given a temporary home in front of the family hotel the Milford Plaza, over the following months, it was visited by thousands of New York residents and tourists, leaving many candles, prayer books and photos of loved ones lost in this appalling tragedy.

Milford Plaza was not a suitable home for the memorial, and for several years, it was placed in storage. The statue now has a permanent home, standing proudly outside the entrance of the Emigrant Savings Bank headquarters at 6 East 43rd Street between 5th and Madison Avenues.

EMIGRANT
SAVINGS
BANK

A FIREFIGHTER'S PRAYER
WHEN I AM CALLED TO DUTY, GOD
WHENEVER FLAMES MAY RAGE, GIVE ME THE STRENGTH
TO SAVE SOME LIFE, WHATEVER BE ITS AGE.

HELP ME EMBRACE A LITTLE CHILD BEFORE IT IS TOO LATE,
OR SAVE SOME OLDER PERSON FROM THE HORROR OF THAT FATE.

ENABLE ME TO BE ALERT AND HEAR THE WEAKEST SHOUT,
AND QUICKLY AND EFFICIENTLY TO PUT THE FIRE OUT.

I WANT TO FILL MY CALLING AND TO GIVE THE BEST IN ME,
TO GUARD MY EVERY NEIGHBOR AND PROTECT HIS PROPERTY.

AND IF I HAVE TO LOSE MY LIFE, ACCORDING TO YOUR WILL,
PLEASE BLESS WITH YOUR PROTECTING HAND
MY CHILDREN AND MY WIFE.

LIN ZE XU

Description:

Bronze 18'.5" high.

This over life-size bronze statue standing on a red granite pedestal was created by the sculptor Li Wei-Si, it was dedicated in 1999 and stands in Chatham Square, East Broadway. Born in Fuzhou, Fujian province of China in 1785 and, despite coming from a poor family with his father's insistence on education he rose through the government.

He was strongly opposed to the opium trade and it was his forceful opposition that led to the First Opium War. He wrote to Queen Victoria asking her to end the opium trade, he pointed out that China was supplying Britain with quality goods, spices, silk, tea and porcelain and Britains sales of opium to China were poisoning the country.

He failed in an attempt to get foreign businesses to exchange their opium stores for tea, after applying force, Captain Charles Elliot, a British government representative ordered all the British traders to hand over their stocks of opium. Great quantities were handed over and 1400 tons were dumped into the sea.

British Pride and business had been offended, the British residents were evacuated. London dispatched an expeditionary force, The First Opium war had begun. The inscription on the pedestal reads, Lin Ze Xu 1785-1850 Pioneer in the War Against Drugs

LIN ZE XU
1785-1850

MOTHER GOOSE

Description:

Height 8'8" (2.64m) width 4'6" (1.37m) depth 5'10" (1.78m) weight 13 tons (13000kg).

This whimsical sculpture by Frederick George Richard Roth was carved by Frederick and his team from a block of Westerly granite in 1936 and dedicated in 1938.

The statue shows a witch sitting on Mother Goose surrounded by Little Jack Horner, Old King Cole, Humpty Dumpty, Old Mother Hubbard and Mary and her Little Lamb all of which we will remember from childhood stories. Frederick Roth was born in Brooklyn in 1872 and studied art in Vienna and at the Academy of Fine art in Berlin, and became a professional sculptor whilst still studying.

One of his first works, the Roman Chariot group, was exhibited in 1901 at the American Exposition in Buffalo New York, it was a great success and created a demand for his artistic and sculptural skills.

In the following years, he created and collaborated on numerous projects and was accepted into many arts organisations. In 1934 he became the chief sculptor for the New York Parks, creating figures from Alice in Wonderland for the Sophie Irene Loeb Fountain near East 76th Street.

NORMAN VINCENT PEALE

Description:

Statue height 8 on base.

Norman Vincent Peale was born on May 31, 1998, his statue was created by John M. Soderberg and dedicated on May 31st outside the Marble Collegiate Church, Sth Avenue & West 29th Street, on what would bave been his 100th birthday.

He was involved with broadcasting on radio and television as well as jourmalisn. He is probably best known for hís best- selling book "The Power of Positive Thínking" published in 1952, hís idea was that nearly all basic problems are personzal.

He was born ín Bowersville, the éldest of thTee sons, hís father was a physician by professign and later became a Methodíst mínister. Peale studicd theology in Boston and during a Summer break served as a pulpit replacenent for a pastor who was taken ill. Whilst still a trainee Peale was persuaded by his father to abandon the formal preaching style he had been taught for one of simplicity.

He kept that philosophy for the rest of his 52 years as pastor of the New York Marble Collegiate Church. Peale officiated at imany prominent weddings including entertainc Lucille Ball to her second husband Gary Morton in 1961 and President Nixon's youngest daughter Julie Nixon to David Eisenhower in 1968.

In 1984 President Ronald Reagan awarded Peale the Presidentíal Medal of Freedom

PEACE FOUNTAIN

Description:

Height 40' (12m) width 13'(3.90m) diameter of pool area 24' (7.30m), pool depth appx. 28" (71.10cm) weight 14 tons (14.22 metric tonnes)

This unusual bronze Fountain was created in 1985 by Gregg Wyatt and represents the eternal conflict between good and evil and is described as 'spiritual realism'.

It can be seen in the West 111th Street People's Garden just south of the Cathedral of St. John the Divine. The curved pedestal made of concrete and stone, represents a double helix of DNA, the building blocks of life, and supports a giant crab representing the origins of life crawling from the sea.

The winged Archangel Michael is wielding his sword, angled towards the ground, having defeated the great evil, Satan whose head is hanging from one of the crab's claws. Below the smiling moon is looking west and on the opposite side, the bright sun is gazing towards the east with a lion and a lamb resting beneath.

A group of nine giraffes represent the most peaceful of animals, one resting its head the on chest of the Archangel. Four flame-like hands are rising from the spiralling eddies of the fountain's base as well as small bronze animals that were sculpted by local school students of all ages, called the Collective Sculpture Garde. The statue no longer functions as a fountain.

PETER PAN

Description:

Height: 59" (149'86 cm) Width 22" (55.88 cm) Depth 22" (55.88 cm)

The bronze statue of Peter Pan, on a circular matt black granite disc with an hexagonal stone base, was created by Charles Andrew Hafner (1889-1960) and cast by A. Ottavino Corporation of New York. Peter Pan is the main character in the world-famous story by the Scottish author Sir James Matthew Barrie, Peter Pan was first seen on stage and turned into a book in 1911 'Peter and Wendy', the story of a boy who never grew up and lived on the island of Never Land with three children from a 'normal' family.

Peter Pan outside of fantasy land led an extraordinary life, in 1928 he was the major figure in a fountain in the lobby of the old Paramount Theater in Times Square which closed after less than 40 years of entertaining the public in 1964.

In 1975, Hugh Trumbull donated the statue to New York City and placed it in Peter's beautiful cloistered garden setting in the Carl Schurz Park along the East River. In August 1999 Peter Pan disappeared, it was nothing to do with fantasy or Captain Hook but simple vandalism.

The New York Police Department searched and eventually found Peter at the bottom of the East River. The half-witted vandals were never found. It was repaired and restored and more securely placed in his garden. Celia Lipton Farris a British actress who had played Peter Pan on stage contributed to the costs of the restoration.

PROMETHEUS WITH FOUNTAIN

Description:

Height 18' (5.5m) and weight 8 tons. Diameter of the fountain basin area 60 by 16' (18.3 by 4.9 m).

This gilded cast bronze figure was created by Paul Manship in 1934 and represents humanity's striving quest for knowledge through the myth of the Titan Prometheus.

He who brought fire to mankind by stealing it from the chariot of the Sun. He was arrested by the Greek God Zeus who punished Prometheus by chaining him to the side of a mountain where he would be eaten by the eagles, but he refused to die and was eventually rescued by Hercules.

The artistic style of this sculpture is known as 'art deco'. It is located in the lower plaza at 45 Rockefeller Centre in Manhattan between 49th and 50th streets off 5th Avenue. The reclining figure hovers over a mountain top clutching a ball of fire in his right hand while being surrounded by a giant ring inscribed with the signs of the zodiac.

The fountain below is a rectangular basin with coloured lights and jets of water streaming upward at different heights in rhythmic patterns. The entire Rockefeller Centre complex is adorned with Art Deco mythological figures representing the activities taking place within the buildings such as radio and television broadcasts as well as other forms of mass media communication.

ROBERT BURNS

Description:

Height 14'10" (452.12cm) 10'square (304.80 cm)

The bronze statue of Robert Burns seated on a tree stump gazing at the heavens, thinking of his one true love Mary Campbell who died whilst still young, a scroll at his feet is inscribed, To Mary in Heaven. The statue is on a pedestal with a brick core and a granite facing. The sculptor was Sir John Steell and cast in 1880.

It was gifted to the city by the Saint Andrews Society of the State of New York. Robert Burns is fondly known worldwide as Rabbie Burns, his true name was Robert Burness and at the age of 27 he decided to shorten it.

Robert, 1759-1796, was born in Alloway, Ayrshire in Scotland, the son of a farmer and on the death of his father in 1784 became head of the family. His birthday, January 25th, 'Burns Night' is celebrated in his homeland and throughout the world with a banquet of haggis a Scottish delicacy.

Two years later he published his poems, they were a tremendous success. He left farming behind and moved to Edinburgh. He was never at ease with the attention that success had created. Robert returned to farming, it was not a great success, his life was literature and all that surrounded it.

In 1789 he began working for the Excise Service and moved to Dumfries and lived there until his death of heart disease in 1796. "May long thy hardy sons of toil be blest with health and peace and sweet content".

ROBERT BURNS

ROSCOE CONKLING

Description:

Height 14' 11" (454.66 cm) Width and Depth 10' 4" (314.96 cm) square.

The bronze statue of Roscoe Conkling stands on a Quincy Granite pedestal, it was sculpted by John Quincy Adams Ward and cast by the Henry-Bonnard Bronze Company of New York.

The statue was cast and dedicated in 1823 and may be seen at Madison Avenue and 23rd Street. Conkling (1829-1888) was born in Albany New York.

He studied law under his father and joined the Francis Kerman law practice. In 1850 Conklin was admitted to the bar and became the District Attorney for Oneida County in New York. In 1858 he became the Mayor of Utica New York and entered the world of politics.

He became a congressman (1859-1863) and a senator (1867-1881). Roscoe Conkling was a philanderer and womaniser. He had an affair with the wife of the former Governor of Rhode Island and was chased out of the Governor's house at gunpoint.

In March 1888 the Great Blizzard shut down New York City with drifts up to 50' high, Conkling was working in his office and decided to walk to the warmth of the New York Club on 25th Street, pushing his way through a fearful blizzard, he reached Union Square and collapsed in a snow drift, he died of pneumonia five weeks later. The statue is placed at a spot near where he collapsed.

ROSCOE CONKLING

SAMUEL REA

Description:

Statue 10 (3.05m) Pedestal 3' (0.0913m)

The bronze statue sculpted by Adolph A. Weinman of Samuel Rea an engineer and president of the Pennsylvania Railroad for over 10 years was dedicated in 1930 a year after his death.

The statue in his honour was originally displayed in the original Pennsylvanin station. Ren is possibly best known for backing a proposal by consulting engincer Gustav Lindenthal to build a massive bridge across the Hudson from Jersey City, New Jersey to Manhattan they wera thwarted by the enormous costs of the project.

He later teamed up with Alexander Cassatt the seventh president of the Pennsylyania Railroad, painter Mary Cassatt's brother and Mooked into the possibilities of building tunnels under the Hudson River.

In 1903 under the leadership of Cassatt and Rea, the project began and was completed in 1910, Rea was also known for being responsible for many of the features in the Esch-Cummins Act, through which the railroads were returned to private control in920 after World War I. Statues of Rea and Cassatt were sculpted by Weinman and were on display, opposite each other in the Old Penn Station. Cassatt. The statue of Cassatt is on display at theailroad Museum.

The statue of Samuel Rea is usually displayed at the entrance of 2 Pennsylvania Plaza, but in 2022 was undercover during renovations.

THE FALCONER

Description:

Figure height 12' (3.66m) The cylindrical polished Barre Vermont granite pedestal height 4'7" (1.4m)

The bronze statue of the Falconer was created by the English sculptor George Blackwell Simmonds in 1871 and cast at the Chevalier Clemente Pape foundry in Florence, Italy. The statue was dedicated in 1875.

He was born into the Simmonds and Courage brewery family, his first love was art and he studied in several European countries before settling in Rome for 12 years.

The Falconer, dressed in a theatrical Elizabethan outfit is perched on a natural rock outcrop, his left arm is stretched toward the sky holding a hunting falcon waiting to be released.

The statue can be found south of the 72nd Street transverse road, and east of the park's West Drive. George Blackwell Simmonds was an enthusiastic falconer. The Falconer has not led a happy existence and has frequently been vandalised, 1937 the statue was in danger of hitting the ground, the Park carried out all the necessary repairs.

In 1957 a new falcon was created and attached, ready for flight. It was vandalised again and was removed to prevent further damage. In 1982 a new arm and falcon were cast and fitted and reinstalled in Central Park. In 1995 The Falcon was completely restored by Central Park Conservancy.

THE INDIAN HUNTER

Description:

Height 10' (304.80 cm) Width 5' (152.40 cm) Depth 6' 3" (190.50 cm)

The bronze statue of The Indian Hunter is poised on a polished Rockport granite pedestal. The statue was created by John Quincy Adams Ward and cast by W. A. Amouroux in New York and dedicated in 1869.

A native American hunter, bow and loose arrow in his hand, leaning forward looking for his prey, the food to feed his family. His other hand controlling his retriever dog, eager to bring the kill back to his master. This statue broke the standard of figurative sculptors. Ward travelled to the area where the hunter would have lived and hunted to get the feeling of them in his hear, he wanted the statue to have emotion.

The statue was funded by a group of prominent citizens and patrons and admirers of his work. In 1937, due to vandalism, the bow was replaced and in 1992 the Central Park Conservancy Monuments Program completely restored The Indian Hunter.

This highly regarded statue was displayed at the Paris Exposition in 1867, the following year the Committee of the Indian Hunter Fund presented the statue to the Board of Commissioners of Central Park.

THE PILGRIM

Description:

Statue height 9' and pedestal height 7.5' and 5' 10" square.

The Pilgrim bronze figure was created by the sculptor John Quincy Adams Ward and shows an idealized Puritan male traveller commemorating the arrival of the Pilgrim fathers on Plymouth Rock Massachusetts in 1620.

This wayfaring Mayflower refugee is outfitted in Cavalier style boots, a high buckled belt, a rolling collar and a wide-brimmed steeple hat holding his flintlock rifle and powder flasks and can be found in Central Park at the North side of the East 72nd Street throughway. The pedestal beneath the statue was designed by architect Richard Morris Hunt and comprises of four bas-reliefs representing aspects of the Pilgrims' landing. One panel is a sword sheathed in a Bible.

A second panel is a depiction of the Mayflower. A third panel is a globe, navigational equipment, a spindle of wool, a hammer and anvil. The fourth panel is a quiver of arrows and a machete.

The statue was unveiled and dedicated in 1885 by the New England Society, a 20-block procession of 225 Society members up Fifth Avenue; accompanied by the 7th Regiment Veterans. In later years The Pilgrim was the first of Central Park's statues to be restored when, in 1979, the Central Park Conservancy initiated its ambitious program to restore its collection of statuary.

In 1999 the powder flasks, by now 115 years old, were recast and replaced.

TO COMMEMORATE
THE LANDING OF THE
PILGRIM FATHERS
ON
PLYMOUTH ROCK
DECEMBER 22 1620

ERECTED BY THE
NEW ENGLAND SOCIETY
IN THE CITY OF NEW YORK
1885

WILLIAM CULLEN BRYANT

Description:

Height Statue 6' (1.83m) Marble Canopy Structure with Base flanked by Urns and Balustrade width 50' (15.25m).

A bronze seated statue by Herbert Adams was installed in Bryant Park in 1911 directly behind the Main Branch of the New York Public Library.

Born in Cummington Massachusetts November 3rd 1794 Bryant struggled in his early career with his true love of poetry and the need to earn a living for his family as a small-town lawyer, receiving a law degree in 1815.

Fortunately, his father Peter Bryant, a physician/surgeon, was also a literary enthusiast and was known to forward his son's poetry to professional journals like The North American Review in Boston.

Bryant's writing talent was immediately recognized but it did still take him until 1825 to be able to move to New York City becoming the editor of The New York Review and later The New York Evening Post. Bryant was to become one of the most significant poets in early American literary history.

Typically included among the group of poets referred to as the fireside poets, along with Longfellow, John Greenleaf Whittier, James Russell Lowell, and Oliver Wendell Holmes Sr. All are considered to be among the first American poets whose popularity rivalled that of British poets. Bryant also voiced his concerns that deforestation in the United States would prove disastrous for American agriculture.

WILLIAM HENRY SEWARD

Description:

Height 17' 9" (5.4m) Width 7' 2" (2.18m) Depth 10' 1" (2.18m).

The bronze statue of William Henry Seward sculpted by Randolph Rogers was originally mounted on a red Levante marble and was dedicated in September 1876.

In 2019 the pedestal was replaced with Arno granite which is more suitable for outdoor life. The statue can be seen facing the intersection of Broadway at the southwest corner of Madison Square Park.

He was the first New Yorker to be honoured with a statue in the city. Born into a wealthy, slave-owning family in the village of Florida in Orange County New York. William H. Seward was the United States Secretary of State under Abraham Lincoln from 1861-1869 and brokered the buying of Alaska from Russia in 1867.

Before the American Civil war, he was a major opponent of the spread of slavery. Before this, he had served two terms as the governor of New York (1839-1843). He was responsible for laws being passed improving the rights and opportunities for the black residents without undermining the current process which was already a good education system.

William Henry Seward was a major figure in the early years of the Republican Party.

WILLIAM SHAKESPEARE

Description:

Height including pedestal 17' 11" (17.92m) 8' (2.44m) square.

The bronze statue of English playwright William Shakespeare, The Bard, (1564 - 1616) was created by sculptor John Quincy Adams Ward after a competition was held to decide which artist would receive this great honour.

Funds were raised by holding benefit performances of Shakespeare's plays. The statue, garbed in classical Elizabethan fashion, stands looking West to the side of a circular walkway at the base of Literary Walk on the Mall in Central Park. Shakespeare never had a portrait made of himself during his lifetime. This and any other likeness are based solely on two portraits created posthumously in approximately 1623.

The first portrait being a funerary sculptural bust on the wall of Holy Trinity Church at Stratford-upon-Avon in Warwickshire England created sometime before 1623. The second portrait is an engraving by Martin Droeshout as the title page of the first collection of Shakespeare's plays published in 1623.

In Central Park, a cornerstone was first laid, near 66th street, in 1864 to commemorate the 300th anniversary of Shakespeare's birth. This was removed in 1872 when the newly installed statue received its dedication. The Central Park Conservancy Project has maintained the sculpture's integrity, finishing restoration work as recently as 1995. Goodnight, goodnight parting is such sweet sorrow.

STATEMENT BY THE AUTHOR

Welcome to New York City. There are 800 monuments, around 250 of which are sculptures, within the mighty five boroughs.

This book will usher you through the streets, parks and avenues where these public artworks reside staunchly braving the elements. A brief description of the sculpted subjects and their creators are included for each work.

Although not all inclusive, these 40 statues selected are an excellent starting point for discovering New York outdoor monuments in person or admiration from afar.

Jack Byard

Author